Owo *whats this*:
A GUIDE TO THE FURRY FANDOM

This first edition of OWO *WHATS THIS*: A GUIDE TO THE FURRY FANDOM was published in 2018

Text and some images copyright © 2018 by Avery Miller

This book will go into the public domain on September 25th, 2028

Special thanks to @mudzzzy, @immaseaurchin, @tallfuzzball, @remorgues, all my patreon supporters, and my baes

A tree will be planted for every paperback copy of this book sold

2

Be yourself, unapologetically.

Now let the memes begin...

How to use this book

Owo *whats this?*

Is... Is someone reading this book!? Wuttt. Uwu *rolls around*

Now that I have that out of my system, hello there, my name is Avery, and I will be walking you through the fuzzy and weird world of the Furry Fandom. However, before we can get down to it, you need to know how to use and navigate this book properly!

While I will be covering the very basics of furries, I do assume you know how to read. This may seem counterintuitive, as werewolves are not known for their reading abilities, but trust me, reading is critical.

Throughout this book, you'll come across little notes, just like this one:

> Owo *whats this... it's a note*
> This is an example note.

These annotations will elaborate on the topics in that page, sometimes providing addition vocab or even links to stuff that you may find useful.

This book is intended to be a parody of those "for dummies" books you may see every so often. Plus, I make videos (more about that later), and I thought me making a book called OWO *WHATS THIS* would be pretty amazing.

Such goofy.

What is a furry?

> Owo *whats this... it's a note*
> This book is completely SFW (meaning "safe for work"), so we're only going to be covering SFW topics-- I'm not judging, we're just going to save NSFW stuff for another time. Follow my after dark if you're... pphhff, haha jk jk. lol.

No turning back now dude.

I think I've clearly established that this manuscript was written mostly as a joke-- A furry encyclopedia that you could buy for your parents, for example, so they can decode your strange twitter ramblings[1] is like, the funniest thing I can think of-- but that doesn't mean this book isn't useful! This chapter is going to mostly be serious-- let's make this a productive thing!

---

[1] If you are a parent reading this, remember: you got your kid somehow, you're stuck with them now! Might as well embrace all this!

There's no greater way to start defining what a furry is than to dismiss what you currently may associate with the furry fandom. There are plenty of misunderstandings among people.

A furry can mostly be defined as someone who associates with anthropomorphised animals. A great comparison I've seen is really committed Star Wars fans... But instead of a movie, we're fans of a concept. The term furry can also refer to an anthro-animal character itself (instead of the person who designed the character).

People who are furries typically have what's called a fursona (we'll go into vocab in an upcoming chapter), or their own original furry character. Often this character is a sort of furry version of the person who made it; other times it's an alter ego. It depends on a case-to-case basis, but I think that covers the majority of furries.

Some people dress up as their sona (again, more about this later) while others chose to create art of their character.

That's the gist of it! That's all you need to know about furries in order for us to get started.

Cringe factor

"AHHH, CRINGE. I KNOW CRINGE VERY WELL, MOSTLY BECAUSE I AM THE PHYSICAL EMBODIMENT OF IT."
-AVERY MILLER 2K18

Some people seem to find furries "cringey"-- The concept of someone pretending to be an animal person is very foreign to everyone at the beginning.

The point I'd like to make here is that many think that furries don't have any self-awareness of this "cringey-ness", and I just want to clear the airways and confirm that we do. We just love furry-ing so much that we ignore it! Think about that.

8

I think that's a good start, let's get down to business.

What is an Avery?

Of course! I'm sure you're wondering, who is this "a very miller"? Why are they so "very" miller?

Good question! It's a common mistake, as Avery is actually my name. I know, strange huh?

Anyways, as previously established, my name is Avery Miller. I'm a youth that makes videos for the internetz. One day, I was bored and thinking about what I should make my next video about, and the concept of creating a book sounded pretty cool to me.

A book about furries is just, such a blending of mediums: internet culture and a physical manuscript?! Sign me up!

Also, I've always wanted to write a book, and why not make my first book something that I'll regret making in 10 years. (I try to regret nothing, but I'll probably still be somewhat embarrassed. Hopefully not though, fingers crossed.)

Important Furry Vocab

The furry fandom is a very tight-knit community, and like many communities, it has vocabulary. I feel that an understanding of this vocab is important in order to fully experience the experience of the furry experience. Following is a list I've compiled of various terms and phrases that I have defined to the best of my ability.

(Something here)

When a word or phrase is surrounded by asterisks, it typically symbolises action. For example, if I said *roles around*, it means that I'm rolling around. Sometimes asterisks are also just used for emphasis, but like, that just happens in english normally.

FOR EXAMPLE (AGAIN): HEHE *ROLLS AROUND*

Blep

A lot of furry related words are rather abstract, and this is one of them.

It's hard to describe.

I think I'd say this is the sound someone makes when they stick their tongue out. However, it's typically used whenever. Like, seriously, there is typically no rhyme or reason to when this is used.

FOR EXAMPLE: HI HI HI HI *BLEP*

Fursuit

Something someone wears to become fuzzy wuzzy, uwu *rubs*.

Hehe, let me elaborate on that.

A fursuit is a costume someone wears that makes them look like their fursona. It's often mascot-like, only cuter. They are famously expensive but like, worth it, or so I've been told.
It is not necessary to have a suit in order to be a furry.

FOR EXAMPLE: LOOK AT THAT ADOR-BS FURSUIT

14
Partial

As I just mentioned, fursuits are expensive and often quite a pain to put on, so some people chose to only get/wear a fursuit head, for example.

FOR EXAMPLE: I HAVE A PARTIAL FURSUIT

This is an image of a Majira Strawberry (Majerious Strabus) in its natural habitat. Notice the body pillow on

the left, the fuzziness, and the strawberry like complection. Image used with permission (thanks btw ;3)

Fat fats

Fat fats are fursuit paws that are rather large and fluffy. And floofy. You know them when you see them.

FOR EXAMPLE: HEHE NICE FAT FATS

Owo *whats this... it's a note*
I made a video about some fat fat paws I bought! Scan this QR code to pull up a search page for that video! I mean, I got to plug.

Paw Beans

In the provided picture of my fat fats, you can see multi-colored "paw pads"-- these are also known as paw beans.

This is because they are on paws, and they look like beans.

These are my fat fat paws. Notice the fatness.

FOR EXAMPLE: I'D LOVE TO BE A PAW BEAN

Boop

A boop is when someone taps on your nose, often done to someone when they are wearing a fursuit (consensually mind you, don't go whacking people in the face, most people don't like that). Additionally, **boopi** is the person getting booped, and **booper** refers to (1) the appendage that one uses to boop the boopi or (2) simply the person who does the boop.

FOR EXAMPLE: I BOOPED THE BOOPI, HEHE

Fursona

I've already talked about this previously, but I feel that it is important enough to the fandom for it to be repeated.

A fursona is like a custom furry character that is often a furry version or an alter ego of a person. However, this depends on a case-to-case basis.

FOR EXAMPLE: LUV UR FURSONA UWU

(Insert word here) Boi

Sometimes one will see boi used after a descriptive word or phrase: someone could say "clicky boi" to refer to some object that clicks, like a mouse or pencil. Elaborating further, one could refer to a rainbow as a "color boi". It's important to note that this is gender neutral.

FOR EXAMPLE (AGAIN): LOOK AT THAT GREEN BOI. *(This would probably refer to a plant, or perhaps a frog.)*

Popufur

This typically is used to refer to a furry who has a large social media following. Occasionally I've seen it used as an insult (to suggest someone has an inflated ego), but also may simply quantitate someone's popularity.

FOR EXAMPLE: JACKFILMS IS A POPU-FUR.

:3, Owo, or x3

:3 and other similar emojis are just that-- emojis!

I've had too many confusing experiences with people who weren't aware of internet emojis. (Once a **x3** emoji was confused with "times 3".) This typically leads to awkward conversations, so be sure to make sure your audience is fuzzy enough to understand this "secret furry language".

FOR EXAMPLE: HEHE OWO ;3

Woah. There you go, those vocab words are all you need to understand most furry conversations. Obviously, there are more terms that don't come to mind at the moment, but these are the necessary basics.

Up next: we're going to be talking about a very prevalent part of the fandom, art.

Furry Art

One of the most prevalent parts of the furry fandom is furry art. It's art with someone's sona in it, and it is often very fun to hire an artist to draw your character.

Of course, you can draw your own art! But, now and again, it's fun to see someone else's take on your fursona.

Before we go into specific types of art you can get commissioned, I'd like to walk you through the process of getting a commission. I've made a video about this before, (you know, crosspromo here; I don't want to seem like I'm referring you to some other place all the time instead of explaining stuff myself, but I mean… if you want more details, you can check that video out) mostly because paying an artist to make a drawing for you may be a little nerve racking at first.

Owo *whats this... it's a note*
I made a video about how to get a commission a while back. Scan this QR code to pull up a search page for that video!
More infos are always nice! ;3

Here's a crucial tip for people looking to get commissions: please do not ask for a free drawing. People asking for free art and then complaining when the artist says no is a pretty famous meme.

If you've thought about doing this, it's okay! You can redeem yourself, you know, everyone does silly stuff, monies are hard to come by, but just be sure to cease and desist that ASAP. It creates a really awkward situation for the artist. Art is a skill that requires a lot of practice and time to execute, and artists are just trying to make a honest living.

Of course, the most important part of a commission in my mind is finding the artist to create the art! I typically look on Twitter or other social media sites to locate a talented individual who is willing to take commissions. Another way to go about this is by looking at who has made art for other furries-- maybe you'll find someone with a style you enjoy! This is a fantastic way to start.

I think we should define different types of art you can get commissioned before we continue.

Sketches

A sketch is a sorta quick-and-dirty drawing that is often less detailed than a "finalized commission".

I think most people would be surprised to see how much details sketches often have; if I commissioned a sketch from an artist, it would probably take me several days to draw something so good myself, while they pull if off in just a couple minutes.

A sketch of one gucci boi. Drawing by Mudzy, @Mudzzzy, used with permission.
10/10, 100/100, would look at again.

Busts/Headshots

When I get a new piece of art, the first thing I want to do is show it off, and one of the best ways for a youth such as myself to do that is by setting the commission as my social media profile picture.

Often artists offer commissions that have been optimized for use as online avatars-- these are known as busts or headshots. Headshots are drawings that are typically from the shoulders up to the top of a character.

Of course these don't have to be used a profile pictures-- Really any type of art could be-- but it's a pretty major use case I've seen.

Full body

Full body art is just that-- a full body drawing of your character! These are often more expensive than a bust or sketch because of the extra details that go into the drawing.

The benefits of a full body drawing often make it worth the price-- the finished product can be used as a reference image for future commissions, and if you decide to use it as a online profile picture, you'll have a lot more options on how to crop the image.

Ref Sheets

If you're planning on getting a suit made at some point or purchasing a lot of commissions, you should totally look into a reference sheet.

A reference sheet is a collection of drawings depicting one's fursona from different angles and views in order to fully get across your sona's physical appearance.

Does that make any sense?[2]

Point is, it's a thingy to show how your lil boopi bud looks.

Like full body commissions, ref sheets are often more expensive than busts or sketches because of the extensive details and how multiple drawings are included in this single commission.

Chibi

The word Chibi supposedly means

---

[2] I think the fact that I've been working on writing this book 24/7 for the last couple days is starting to show in my writing.

small in Japanese, and it's a pretty accurate description of this style.

    A Chibi is a type of drawing that is typically less detailed and very stylized. It truly depends on the specific artist who is making the drawing, I think that's a pretty good basis to understand what a Chibi is.

Here we see me trying to be a scary boi. Drawn by my bff @mudzzzy, used with permission.

Traditional Art

Traditional art is art that is drawing physically, typically onto canvas or paper.

The benefit of physical art is that by the end of the whole process, you have something that you can actually hold! I know I personally love this sort of thing.

Of course, because physical materials are being used, it typically costs a lot more than the typical digital drawing, but can totally be worth it, just depends on what you're looking for.

On the next page, we see a spooky drawing of me done on paper and scanned into the computerz. Drawn by the talented @immaseaurchin, used with permission.

As far as I know, those are the most common types of commissions you'll come across!

Now that you know how to describe what type of commission you're looking for, you need to reach out to that artist you found earlier! You'll want to describe what you're looking for, and ask about prices. I personally have a problem with patience (hence this book being written in a couple days lol), so it's really important to not try to bug the artist too much-- they could be busy or maybe even not currently taking commissions.

Just in case they aren't taking commissions, I'd recommend having a backup artist lined up ;3

Throw in some waiting and that's all there is to it!

A Brief Fursuit Introduction

I have a confession to make.

In my years of being in the fandom, I've mostly only participated in the digital-side of furrieness: art, making videos, that sorta stuff. I haven't until relatively recently dabbled in the cosplay aspect of furries-- fursuiting.

Why did it take so long? I think it's mainly because of the cost of fursuits. A nice suit can get over $1000 easy. That might seem like a lot, but when you look at the materials and how much time and care goes into making a suit, it becomes evident to where that money goes.

There is a common misconception that all furries are fursuiters (obviously, you don't need a suit to be a furry), and although this is nothing more than a misconception, I think it's sorta made me look into suiting. As a furry, lots of people expect you to dress up, and if you don't, the "taboo" of being a fursuiter is there, but without actually fursuiting, so you're like, missing out?! Does that make sense?

Basically, I said I might as well try it. There's nothing to lose :3

So, I got some fat fat paws (as seen in a previous chapter) and can I just say that I understand why people cosplay as their sona-- there is just something about it that I think you have to experience to fully grasp.

It makes you feel cute, and if you're interested in the fandom, I invite you to give some aspect of cosplaying a try, you might as well!

35
Life Hacks from Avery

Before we get all wrapped up here with this beginner's guide to the fandom, I thought I'd give you some additional tips from someone who has been a furry for a number of years, and I think we should start with the freaky one!

Be careful of spooks

Chances are, every so often you'll come across a mean furry. Often people can lash out at each other over disagreements on certain topics, and I'm not necessarily talking about people who do that.[3] We're talking about people who are repeatedly a jerk, people who seem to have controversy follow them around often. (I've always found

---
[3] I think most people are guilty of that sorta thing now and again.

this strange considering how much of a happy, loving group furries tend to be.)

For our purposes I'd categorize these people into two groups: (1) someone who is a bit of a meanie, may say some hurtful stuff, but when it comes to it, they can mostly just be ignored without much consequence or (2) someone who says really bad, really stupid, not cool stuff, to the point that it starts to negatively affect the image of the fandom. With the latter case, furries are often compelled to publicly condemn that 2nd category person, in fear of getting grouped together with them; I know what comes to mind for me are neo-nazis.

I'm serious. Furries with neo-nazi ties[4]. It's one of the most ridiculous things I've ever seen, so like, keep a look out for people like that, they are bad.

---

[4] Love and equality is what the fandom is about, if you're a nazi you don't get to be a furry.

37
Be chill, have fun!

My last piece of advice is to chill and have fun. Be weird, be cute.

This book started as a joke, and tbh still is, but at the same time, there is some real truth here.

Stay fuzzy, and see you on the internet.

<3avery

Made in the USA
San Bernardino, CA
08 August 2020